Foreword／はじめに

For the past decade, I have been trying to develop improved forms of TOEIC® L&R instruction that will better benefit students and help them achieve higher scores on the TOEIC® L&R Test. With reading, the answer for improving your score is simple: you must practice, practice, practice. The reading questions in this book were written with a specific level and situation (travel, hotels, office) in mind. This is to help students anticipate the content and read problems aimed at their English level. This sh[...]en motivate students to practice further. Doing this is [...] improve one's TOEIC® L&R reading ability.

Matthew Wilson

TOEIC® L&R リーディングスコアアップのためには、基礎的な文法力と語彙力、そして TOEIC® L&R の形式を知り慣れることが大切です。本書はそれらの能力を総合的に高めることを目的に編集されていますので、この一冊を繰り返しやるだけでも TOEIC® L&R に求められる文法力と語彙力、そして頻出問題のシーンやパターンを知ることが可能です。問題に取り組むときは、書かれている状況を推測しながら読み進めましょう。パート５とパート６の文法、語彙問題は繰り返し問題を解いてください。パート６の文章挿入問題とパート７は、本文の中に必ず答えを見つけるための手がかりがあるはずです。解法のためのプロセスが本書を通して見えてくるはずです。

鶴岡　公幸

英語はスポーツと同じです。サッカーで勝つために、基本のドリブル練習や、実践での練習試合を重ねるのと同様に、TOEIC® L&R のリーディングスコアアップにも、「語彙力」と「文法力」の基本のルールを覚え、実際に「解く」実践トレーニングが必須です。本書では、最新の『頻出語彙問題』、『頻出文法問題』で基礎を固めながら、『出題パターンに慣れる』実践練習が可能です。また、TOEIC® L&R のリーディングセクションでは、限りある制限時間を上手に配分し、得意なテーマの問題でより得点を獲ることが鍵となります。本書は、頻出テーマに分かれているため、自分が得意なテーマ、苦手なテーマを知ることができます。学習は、自分の弱点を知ることから始まります。学習後には、復習するべき項目が明確になるはずです。本書が、多くの方の TOEIC® L&R スコアアップ、英語力向上に役立つことを願っています。

佐藤　千春

Business World

Part 5

Incomplete Sentences

Select the best answer to complete the sentence. Then choose the letter (A), (B), (C), or (D).

1. That company used to ------- the computer software market.

   (A) hit   (B) secure   (C) update   (D) corner

2. This new way of ------- large machinery will help cut costs.

   (A) dismantled   (B) dismantles   (C) dismantling   (D) dismantle

3. Plastic can cause a ------- amount of harm, not only to the environment but also to humans.

   (A) big   (B) full   (C) substantial   (D) little

4. We can give you an additional seven-days ------- on the loan payment.

   (A) extend   (B) extensive   (C) extension   (D) extending

5. If you're already signed into the account, ------- you'll automatically be signed out when the transaction is complete.

   (A) until   (B) additional   (C) then   (D) though

6. ------- you have installed the new software, you cannot use the previous version.

   (A) Despite   (B) During   (C) While   (D) Once

7. The restaurant -------- featured on that TV show, eventually used it as PR.

   (A) prominence   (B) prominently   (C) prominences   (D) prominent

8. You should erase the hard drive ------- you sell your computer.

   (A) ahead   (B) before   (C) previous   (D) former

Part 6

Text Completion

Select the best answer to complete the text. Then choose the letter (A), (B), (C), or (D).

Questions 9-12 refer to the following advertisement.

Having trouble getting the right person for the job? Find qualified ------
9.
fast with Catch Recruiter. Our customizable templates make it easy to
write your job description. Then, we send your job posting out to 100+ of
the top job sites. Our powerful matching technology scans thousands of
resumes to find people with the right skills, education, and experience ------
10.
your job, then actively invites them to apply to your company. It's all so ------.
11.
------. After that, decide if we are the right match for you.
12.

9. (A) candidates   (B) nominees   (C) entrants   (D) contestants

10. (A) to   (B) with   (C) for   (D) at

11. (A) ease   (B) easy   (C) easier   (D) easiest

12. (A) Send us your most recent resume ASAP.
   (B) Our rates are reasonable, but you must act fast.
   (C) This time of year we are incredibly busy.
   (D) Try a free 14-day trial to see if you like us.

Reading Comprehension

Select the best answer for each question and mark the letter (A), (B), (C), or (D).

Questions 13-14 refer to the following website form.

https://www.sportsworld.com/

Thank you for choosing Sportsworld.com, the world's leading web page for connecting sellers and buyers of new and used sports equipment. Please fill out the information below, and it will be posted on our website!

VENDOR INFORMATION

Company name: Spring Sports Office
Address: 2109 West
City, State, ZIP code: Pensacola, FL, 87600
Phone NO: 506-567-2110
E-mail: sportsworld@com

DESCRIPTION OF EQUIPMENT

Category: Baseball
Equipment: Left-handed glove (new, used)
Model: MB-1290
Condition: Standard
Price: $350

13. Who might be interested in this service?

(A) Website designers

(B) Sports equipment manufacturers

(C) Sellers of office equipment

(D) Buyers of sports equipment

14. For this order, what could be said about the equipment?

(A) It's in average condition.

(B) It's in exceptional condition.

(C) It's in poor condition.

(D) The condition is unknown.

Questions 15-17 refer to the following letter.

To Whom It May Concern:

In the shipment of 12 boxes of Scandinavian wine glasses, dated October 20 from your Stockholm warehouse, 4 boxes were found to have broken glasses. While 8 boxes were properly packed with cardboard dividers and plastic wrapping around each glass, 4 boxes lacked these cardboard dividers. The glasses were packed with only the plastic wrappers around them and nothing to hold them in place when the box was carried. In total, 48 of the 144 glasses shipped in those boxes were broken.

Photographic evidence of the damage is included. As these boxes were not shipped under normal packing procedure, we expect they will be replaced at your expense. Please ship the replacements immediately as our inventory is very low at the moment.

Thank you,
Pete Schweddy
The Glass House

15. What is the purpose of this letter?
- (A) To cancel a Scandinavian tour
- (B) To inform of an incorrect order
- (C) To inquire about a shipping delay
- (D) To report a poorly prepared package

16. What has been enclosed with this letter?
- (A) A receipt
- (B) An inventory checklist
- (C) Directions to a warehouse
- (D) A photo

17. What is requested in the letter?
- (A) A full refund
- (B) A second shipment
- (C) Free gift wrapping
- (D) Complimentary wine

Education

Part 5

Incomplete Sentences

Select the best answer to complete the sentence. Then choose the letter (A), (B), (C), or (D).

1. To register for a bicycle parking permit, fill in the ------- form.

   (A) applicant   (B) application   (C) apply   (D) applied

2. We have to try ------- all possible incorrect answers first.

   (A) elimination   (B) eliminate   (C) eliminating   (D) eliminated

3. In order to get ------- degree, he had to pass the final exam.

   (A) he   (B) him   (C) himself   (D) his

4. ------- the report, students at that medical school undergo very intensive training.

   (A) As opposed to   (B) In addition to   (C) According to   (D) Prior to

5. The school ------- her tuition because she got a high GPA last semester.

   (A) abandoned   (B) left   (C) waived   (D) resigned

6. The information about summer internships is ------- to change without notice.

   (A) capable   (B) used   (C) back   (D) subject

7. He was an ------- scholar of Shakespeare's works.

   (A) accomplishment   (B) accomplish   (C) accomplished   (D) accomplishing

8. ------- there is a special reason, the midterm exam can be held in the big auditorium.

   (A) If   (B) Eventually   (C) Despite   (D) What

Part 6

Text Completion

Select the best answer to complete the text. Then choose the letter (A), (B), (C), or (D).

Questions 9-12 refer to the following web page.

From funding scholarships and research to creating world-class ------, **9.** donations to Winnipeg University (WU) help make it one of Canada's leading institutions. Our donation program allows you two ways to pay. A one-time donation that ------ your money is invested in long-term projects and programs **10.** at WU that benefit students. ------, by choosing a long-term donation schedule, **11.** you can decide when and how often you would like to give money. ------. **12.** Whichever you choose, your generosity is helping to create a new generation of leaders who will not only go on to change their community, but also the world.

9. (A) materials   (B) appliances   (C) facilities   (D) comforts

10. (A) ensure   (B) ensures   (C) ensuring   (D) ensured

11. (A) Differently   (B) Even though   (C) On the other hand   (D) At any rate

12. (A) Information about courses of study can be found in the menu.
    (B) The university prefers fewer payments but larger dollar amounts.
    (C) Failing to achieve our financial goal, will put WU's future in danger.
    (D) Payments can be in easy monthly, quarterly, or annual installments.

Part 7

Reading Comprehension

Select the best answer for each question and mark the letter (A), (B), (C), or (D).

Questions 13-14 refer to the following website.

https://www.bloomingtonps.com/

Bloomington Public Schools

Computer Science Education

We are preparing students to thrive in a rapidly changing world. While it is hard to predict the jobs of tomorrow, we know critical thinking, creativity, and problem-solving skills are in-demand for the 21st century workplace. Our curriculum has been carefully designed to meet parents' requests and provides these computer science concepts in subjects throughout their school experience.

You will be happy to learn that we are also expanding the Computer Science instruction available to students. Our high schools offer Computer Science, and a developing computer science pathway that begins in elementary school and will continue through middle school and high school.

13. Who are the intended readers?

(A) Elementary school children

(B) Parents of school children

(C) University students

(D) Business people

14. What is NOT mentioned in their curriculum?

(A) Critical thinking

(B) Creativity

(C) Inter-personal skills

(D) Problem-solving skills

Questions 15-16 refer to the following book review.

Convincing your children to do things they *don't* want to do can be challenging. And making them stop doing the things you don't want them to do can be even trickier still.

Author Dr. Kennedy asked experts who have cracked the code of what does (and doesn't) drive kids to improve their behavior to share their wisdom. Running through this book, you can understand that the key to motivating kids is different than what was commonly thought. The chapters of the book are as follows:

#1- Reconsider Rewards
#2- Have Meaningful Conversations
#3- Embrace Their Imperfections
#4- Consider Their Capabilities
#5- Express Appreciation

15. **What most likely would be the title of this book?**

   (A) Your Child Will Never Change

   (B) Ways to Motivate Your Kids

   (C) Bad Children Are Fine

   (D) Children Are a Mirror of You

16. **Which chapter would most likely touch upon the topic of "how to thank your child"?**

   (A) Chapter 1

   (B) Chapter 3

   (C) Chapter 4

   (D) Chapter 5

Scene **3**

Daily Life

Part 5

Incomplete Sentences

Select the best answer to complete the sentence. Then choose the letter (A), (B), (C), or (D).

1. The Safety Guide explains the measures taken to ensure the safety of ------- during an emergency.

   (A) commuted   (B) commute   (C) commuting   (D) commuters

2. The grocery shop near my house has a good ------- for quality and value.

   (A) retail   (B) notice   (C) reputation   (D) information

3. The cost of renting a ------- apartment varies depending on the size and the location.

   (A) furnished   (B) furniture   (C) furnishing   (D) furnish

4. If you notice a passenger feeling ill, please ------- the station staff or a guard nearby.

   (A) explain   (B) talk   (C) accompany   (D) notify

5. It has been ------- more economical to use electronic payment apps to buy things.

   (A) much   (B) very   (C) rarely   (D) so

6. Games for smartphones have become popular ------- sales of software for other games are declining.

   (A) now that   (B) only if   (C) while   (D) whether

7. When the customer complained about the broken item, the salesperson ------- and offered to replace it.

   (A) behaved   (B) asserted   (C) apologized   (D) excused

8. Only ------- of that city are eligible to enter the contest.

   (A) resident   (B) residents   (C) residences   (D) residential

Part 6

Text Completion

Select the best answer to complete the text. Then choose the letter (A), (B), (C), or (D).

Questions 9-12 refer to the following notice.

------- the recent virus outbreak, all branches of the library will be closed until
9.

further notice. Our online resources will remain available and Wi-Fi capabilities

will extend ------- our parking lot. Please do not return materials at this time.
10.

You will not be charged late -------. Learn about changes to library services and
11.

policies in response to the current situation online: www.american.edu/library/

virus.

-------. Stay safe everyone!
12.

9. (A) Though   (B) Due to   (C) While   (D) Since

10. (A) into   (B) by   (C) for   (D) at

11. (A) money   (B) bill   (C) costs   (D) fees

12. (A) Ask about updates to policies at our reception desk.
    (B) DVDs and CDs need to be returned as usual.
    (C) A list of upcoming events can be found online.
    (D) We thank you for your cooperation.

Reading Comprehension

Select the best answer for each question and mark the letter (A), (B), (C), or (D).

Questions 13-14 refer to the following notice.

Dear users,

A wallet was found on the floor of this laundromat early Sunday morning with the inscription G.W. It doesn't contain any money or I. D. with an address or phone number. In the wallet, there are several photos, a blood donor's card and medical results for Jiro, which is probably a pet. If this is your wallet or you have any information about the owner, please contact our office: 050 5150 5555

13. What was found on Sunday?

(A) A lost pet

(B) Some laundry

(C) A personal belonging

(D) A phone

14. Who might read this notice?

(A) Blood donors

(B) Laundry users

(C) Pet owners

(D) The family of G.W.

Please come to our spring garage sale! We will put many items in front of our apartment complex for you to look around. Lots of clothing, used books & magazines, toys, furniture, kitchen goods and electric devices will be there. Things are not free, but very affordable for what they probably cost in stores. Please stop by from 10:00-18:00 this Friday and Saturday.

15. What would mostly likely NOT be found at this sale?

(A) Old televisions

(B) Table tennis rackets

(C) A bookshelf

(D) A kitchen blender

16. What are people told to expect about the prices?

(A) They'll be expensive.

(B) They'll be 10% off of the market price.

(C) They'll be reasonable.

(D) They'll depend on the item.

Health

Part 5

Incomplete Sentences

Select the best answer to complete the sentence. Then choose the letter (A), (B), (C), or (D).

1. You should come back to the hospital ------- if your symptoms worsen.

   (A) dramatically   (B) immediately   (C) critically   (D) concisely

2. As a leading ------- company, we try to develop innovative products.

   (A) pharmacy   (B) pharmacist   (C) pharmaceutical   (D) pharmacists

3. It is important to ------- your medicine before you completely run out.

   (A) pack   (B) show   (C) work   (D) refill

4. We recommend you ------- a letter from your family doctor.

   (A) bring   (B) brought   (C) to bring   (D) bringing

5. A fever and a sore throat can be an initial ------- of many illnesses.

   (A) aspect   (B) symptom   (C) caution   (D) detail

6. You'll get high blood pressure ------- you get more exercise and eat healthier.

   (A) unless   (B) until   (C) although   (D) however

7. Dr. White advised his patients to see a ------- about their diets.

   (A) nutrition   (B) nutritionist (C) nutritional   (D) nutritious

8. ------- an emergency, please dial 911 for an ambulance.

   (A) When   (B) In case of   (C) Due to   (D) Instead of

Text Completion

Select the best answer to complete the text. Then choose the letter (A), (B), (C), or (D).

Questions 9-12 refer to the following internal memo.

Hello everyone,

More information from me about our company's new health and wellness initiatives. Our monthly *Panther Newsletter* will become an ------ way to provide
9.
wellness content to employees. It won't only have a few wellness articles. There will now be a permanent section in the newsletter ------ devoted to wellness
10.
content. This will be about anything health ------ such as nutrition, running,
11.
walking, healthy recipes, and so on. We'll keep copies of the newsletter in the break room as well as work areas, so it's readily available for you to pick up and read. ------. We encourage you to share the information with friends and family.
12.

More ideas to come!

Peter Sellers
CEO, Panther, Inc.

---

9. (A) effect   (B) effecting   (C) effective   (D) effectiveness

10. (A) individually   (B) precisely   (C) exactly   (D) solely

11. (A) related   (B) attached   (C) linked   (D) pertinent

12. (A) We are currently asking for submissions for the newsletter.
   (B) Health and wellness goals are to be set by each employee.
   (C) If the content appeals to you, just take the newsletter home.
   (D) Subscription prices for the newsletter have yet to be decided.

Part 7

Reading Comprehension

Select the best answer for each question and mark the letter (A), (B), (C), or (D).

Questions 13-14 refer to the following article.

Traveling on an airplane for over 8 hours can lead to problems like blood clots in legs. Cramped seating, inactivity, and dehydration associated with air travel all increase the risk of blood clotting in the legs. If a large clot moves to the lungs or brain, a person can lose their life. The best travel tips for long flights are:

1: Have leg space: sit by an exit or the aisle so you can stretch your legs.

2: Hydrate: drink lots of water and avoid alcohol.

3: Move: try to walk in the aisle for a few minutes once every hour.

4: Take off shoes: Move your toes, massage your feet, and stretch your legs.

13. How can blood clots develop on long flights?

(A) From too much sleep

(B) From eating too much

(C) From drinking too much

(D) From inactivity and dehydration

14. How often should a passenger on a long trip try to walk?

(A) Every 15 minutes

(B) Every 30 minutes

(C) Every 45 minutes

(D) Every 60 minutes

Questions 15-16 refer to the following announcement.

Stress Management Workshop

Are you stressed, burned out and tired at work? Do you suffer from chronic pain? If so, you should attend the special workshop with Dr. Dick Stewart, internationally renowned expert on stress management.

Time: Friday, November 3, 1-2:30 P.M.
Place: Oaks Hotel, Room B

Dr. Stewart will discuss and teach attendees his methods for reducing stress. These methods have been shown to be successful in many different cases. In his workshop, attendees will learn techniques for neck and shoulder stress, and learn how to cope with stress inducing factors such as workplace arguments, relationships, working with difficult people and strict deadlines.

Interested parties should contact 877-455-0009 for reservations and further information.

15. What are some causes of stress?

  (A) Drinking alcohol

  (B) Dealing with certain people

  (C) Having meals with family members

  (D) Excessive exercise

16. Who would most likely be interested in this workshop?

  (A) Summer interns

  (B) Hotel owners

  (C) Office managers

  (D) New employees

Scene 5

Job Interviews

Part 5

Incomplete Sentences

Select the best answer to complete the sentence. Then choose the letter (A), (B), (C), or (D).

1. Each department's hiring managers are ------- for their recruitment.

   (A) respective   (B) ideal   (C) temporary   (D) responsible

2. James got ------- to Vice-President this year.

   (A) promoted   (B) to promote   (C) promoting   (D) promote

3. When you fill ------- the form, please write legibly and accurately.

   (A) for   (B) to   (C) down   (D) in

4. She was 22 years old when she ------- her father in running the family company.

   (A) succeeds   (B) successes   (C) successful   (D) succeeded

5. ------- Jennifer worked full-time, she wasn't entitled to work benefits.

   (A) Although   (B) Instead   (C) Despite   (D) Otherwise

6. This new job posting system enables us to develop ------- human resources.

   (A) complicated   (B) capable   (C) unqualified   (D) efficient

7. We can provide you a letter of ------- if need be.

   (A) recommends   (B) recommending   (C) recommendation   (D) recommended

8. Qualified candidates will be offered a position ------- following the interview.

   (A) sensitively   (B) extremely   (C) immediately   (D) figuratively

Text Completion

Select the best answer to complete the text. Then choose the letter (A), (B), (C), or (D).

Questions 9-12 refer to the following e-mail.

Date: Monday, July 6

Subject: Inquiry

Dear Carole Swift,

I am currently researching positions in the field of public relations. Tim Murphy at WaterMelon Design ------- that you would be an excellent source of
9.
information and that I should contact you.

As you will see from the enclosed resume, my education and work experience are in marketing. I would like to transfer the skills that I ------- over the years to a
10.
job in public relations.

-------, I hope that you can find 30 minutes to meet with me before the end of
11.
the month. I plan to contact you again to set up an appointment by the end of the week. -------.
12.

If you have questions, please contact me by e-mail.

I appreciate your time in considering my request.

Sincerely,

Jill Ferrell

9. (A) predicted   (B) reminded   (C) communicated   (D) suggested

10. (A) acquire   (B) acquiring   (C) am acquiring   (D) have acquired

11. (A) At last   (B) After all   (C) In closing   (D) In the end

12. (A) I'll come to your office in person to discuss the account.
     (B) I fail to understand why you would refuse to hire me.
     (C) Forgive me if I seem too forward with this request.
     (D) I strongly recommend that you hire Tim Murphy.

Reading Comprehension

Select the best answer for each question and mark the letter (A), (B), (C), or (D).

Questions 13-14 refer to the following letter.

Dear Mr. Dawson,

Enclosed is the resume you requested detailing my experience in the fields of marketing and advertising. As you will see, I have worked in many areas like public relations, consumer electronics, and IT.

I'm convinced I can contribute to your company with all my experience and because of our shared marketing values that came up over our discussion on the phone the other day.

I will contact you next week and hopefully we can meet to discuss specifically how I can assist you and your company in expanding your current market share.

If you have any questions, please feel free to call or e-mail me anytime.

Sincerely,
Shin Taguchi
905-777-8679
staguchi@geemail.com

---

13. What is the purpose of this letter?

    (A) To recommend hiring a coworker

    (B) To market himself further

    (C) To request a letter of reference

    (D) To reschedule a meeting

14. What experience does Mr. Taguchi NOT have?

    (A) Public Relations

    (B) Accounting

    (C) Advertising

    (D) Information Technology

Questions 15-16 refer to the following e-mail.

TO: sjohnson@citysportsclub.org
FROM: akemper@wellnesscenter.com

Hi Steve,

Thank you for all your help last month. I'm always impressed with how well you work with children. The kids enjoyed having you teach them how to swim. Later this summer, we'll be teaching another group of about 15 children how to swim before they head off to summer camp. Would you be interested in volunteering your time and expertise? It'll only be two days (July 27 and July 28), and meals and transportation will be provided, of course. If you're busy, that's OK. I have another instructor in mind, but thought I'd contact you first.

To be honest, many kids have asked me, "Is Mr. Johnston going to teach us?" Apparently, you have a good reputation and the kids are all telling each other about you!

Thanks again for your help and I look forward to your reply.

Best wishes,
Amanda Kemper
Wellness Center

15. **What will Ms. Kemper do if Mr. Johnson is unavailable?**

    (A) She'll find another instructor.
    (B) She'll cancel the class.
    (C) She'll teach it herself.
    (D) She'll reschedule the times.

16. **Why does Ms. Kemper want Mr. Johnson to teach the children?**

    (A) He's the only certified instructor.
    (B) He's a famous swimmer.
    (C) She needs a summer camp instructor.
    (D) He's popular with the children.

Meetings

Part 5

Incomplete Sentences

Select the best answer to complete the sentence. Then choose the letter (A), (B), (C), or (D).

1. Please turn off your phones so they don't ------- the presentation.

   (A) interrupt   (B) object   (C) mention   (D) end

2. According to a full ------- of the schedule, a winter launch would be ideal.

   (A) analyze   (B) analytical   (C) analysis   (D) analyst

3. The team's performance has improved ------- he became the manager.

   (A) for   (B) during   (C) since   (D) while

4. The CEO's speech was ------- similar to last year's.

   (A) striking   (B) strike   (C) stroked   (D) strikingly

5. The director was forced to explain the problems -------.

   (A) himself   (B) yourselves   (C) itself   (D) ourselves

6. We should not leave this important decision to another person's -------.

   (A) hand   (B) discretion   (C) theme   (D) persuasion

7. The documents you discuss at the meeting should be given ------- e-mailed in advance.

   (A) or   (B) for   (C) what   (D) since

8. Please propose a few dates ------- are convenient for you.

   (A) what   (B) when   (C) that   (D) this

Text Completion

Select the best answer to complete the text. Then choose the letter (A), (B), (C), or (D).

Questions 9-12 refer to the following e-mail.

From: tedtanaka@ntvcommunications.com

To: staff@ntvcommunications.com

Date: Tuesday, May 12

Subject: Meeting Follow-up

Greetings,

Here's the follow-up for our department meeting yesterday. Attached are the meeting's ------. As always, thank you, Claire, for preparing them.
9.

To ------ the main points that came up in the meeting:
10.

· To reduce paper waste, the company newsletter will become a bimonthly publication.

· A proposal for standing desk requests will ------ to head office.
11.

· Those interested in being an office buddy for summer interns need to talk to Kate.

------. For absentees, it is important that you become familiar with the content of
12.

the attachment and reply to me with any questions or concerns you may have.

Thank you.

Ted Tanaka

---

9. (A) seconds   (B) minutes   (C) hours   (D) times

10. (A) result   (B) respond   (C) realize   (D) recap

11. (A) submit   (B) submitted   (C) submits   (D) be submitted

12. (A) Quite a few of you were unable to attend yesterday.
    (B) It is too late if you disagree with the above ideas.
    (C) Please find time to thank Claire for her effort.
    (D) If there is a mistake in the attachment, inform Kate.

Select the best answer for each question and mark the letter (A), (B), (C), or (D).

Questions 13-14 refer to the following letter.

Dear Mr. Seiji Akiyama,

I'm Daniel Saito, and I work in the Research & Development Department at Boston Marketing. We're specialists in helping our clients start Internet advertising campaigns. Given that you're one of the leading toiletry companies within the same niche market as us, I believe a collaboration would be in both our interests. Working together, you'd benefit from access to our consulting team and our Internet advertising platforms.

I'd like to take this opportunity to invite you to a special seminar detailing this opportunity at Tokyo Spring Hotel, April 15 from 13:00 to 15:00. We can discuss things further at that time.

Kind regards,

Daniel Saito

Boston Marketing

13. What is the purpose of this letter?

(A) To sell a product

(B) To inform of a seminar

(C) To propose a company merger

(D) To hold a joint seminar

14. What specialty does Boston Marketing offer?

(A) Renting spaces

(B) Writing articles

(C) Developing shopping malls

(D) Providing consulting services

Dear Ms. Smith,

Thank you for taking time out of your busy schedule to meet with me last Thursday afternoon. Although our time was somewhat limited, I felt I was able to explain what our products can do for your company.

Additionally, I want to stress that we can provide same-day delivery for all our products if those products are ordered before noon. Also, if you place orders which exceed the quantities on the price list, we are willing to adjust the price accordingly.

If you have any questions regarding our company and products, please don't hesitate to call me anytime from 9:00 a.m. to 5:00 p.m.

Thank you for your attention.

Tomas Clerk

15. **What is the purpose of this letter?**
    (A) An apology
    (B) A business idea proposal
    (C) A follow-up
    (D) A letter of reference

16. **When is the deadline for the same-day delivery?**
    (A) 9:00 A.M.
    (B) 10:00 A.M.
    (C) 12:00 noon
    (D) 5:00 P.M.

Money

Part 5

Incomplete Sentences

Select the best answer to complete the sentence. Then choose the letter (A), (B), (C), or (D).

1. Customers can cancel their tickets and demand reimbursement ------- 24 hours of their purchases.

    (A) even   (B) within   (C) above   (D) when

2. Many students undertake part-time jobs and find it is a great way to earn some ------- money.

    (A) extra   (B) small   (C) quite   (D) well

3. This kind of business will be very ------- in the next few years.

    (A) profitably   (B) profitability   (C) profitable   (D) profit

4. The charges for the hotel room, which came to $200 a night, were a little more expensive ------- expected.

    (A) than   (B) but   (C) above   (D) over

5. Mr. Smith has worked as an ------- for our company for the past 10 years.

    (A) accountant   (B) account   (C) accounting   (D) accounts

6. ------- the leaders voted to improve family benefits on Wednesday, it's not yet decided.

    (A) As soon as   (B) So that   (C) Rather than   (D) Although

7. The company ------- a large amount of money to my fundraiser.

    (A) conducted   (B) contributed   (C) acquired   (D) counted

8. The committee implemented an analysis of food -------.

    (A) expending   (B) expenditures   (C) expend   (D) expended

Part 6

Text Completion

Select the best answer to complete the text. Then choose the letter (A), (B), (C), or (D).

Questions 9-12 refer to the following article.

New Bank Notes Are Safer, Sturdier and Better for Environment

The new euro bank notes introduced on Tuesday, were made to be easier to handle and more resistant to illegal copying. Shinier and with more security features, these new notes are more durable than their ------. They are also
9.
vegan ------, unlike the previous bills. A spokeswoman for the European
10.
Central Bank said that there was no evidence of any animal-based products in the new bill's raw materials. "The paper we use in the bank notes ------
11.
of 100 percent cotton fiber," she said, adding, "------." The spokeswoman also
12.
emphasized that, "The euro system is trying hard to maintain the sustainability of these new euro bank notes for years to come."

9. (A) ancestors   (B) descendants   (C) founders   (D) predecessors

10. (A) friend   (B) friendly   (C) friends   (D) friendship

11. (A) make   (B) making   (C) has made   (D) is made

12. (A) The old notes are now collectors' items that may increase in value.
    (B) We're committed to improving the raw materials used to make them.
    (C) There have been many people who are against these new policies.
    (D) It is said that we may return to old methods if the economy worsens.

Reading Comprehension

Select the best answer for each question and mark the letter (A), (B), (C), or (D).

Questions 13-14 refer to the following excerpt.

Q: I want to save money for my retirement but I have a little concern. As I work as a freelance photographer at different firms, my income varies each month. It means I can deposit a lot into my Individual Retirement Account some months and nothing at all some months. How can I invest money consistently?

A: There are many investors like you who find it difficult to be consistent. The recommended plan for people in your position is to have a direct deposit plan. This way, your IRA fund takes a small portion from every paycheck. Most investors don't notice the difference after a few paychecks and watch as their IRA funds slowly but steadily build up.

---

13. What is the objective of the person who wrote the question?

(A) To invest regularly
(B) To find an appropriate bank
(C) To spend money wisely
(D) To share money with family

14. What is the advantage of a direct deposit plan?

(A) It helps people who are too busy to invest.
(B) It gets a good interest rate from the bank.
(C) It is a consistent way to save money.
(D) It can fully maximize assets.

Socially responsible investing has been a recently popular term that reflects one's beliefs, philosophies, and values, beyond making a financial benefit.

In the past decade, many investors learned that they were indirectly supporting companies whose activities conflict with their profit. To solve this contradiction, consulting firms are emerging to provide information about socially responsible company models. Using this information, investors can make sure that their invested money is used toward causes they agree with.

15. Who provides the information about socially responsible companies?

(A) Consulting firms

(B) Investment banks

(C) Green companies

(D) Non-profit organizations

16. The word "causes" in paragraph 2, line 7, is closet in meaning to

(A) results

(B) aims

(C) reasons

(D) perspectives

Office Life

Part 5

Incomplete Sentences

Select the best answer to complete the sentence. Then choose the letter (A), (B), (C), or (D).

1. To keep your system running well, you need to install the latest ------- software.

   (A) secure   (B) secured   (C) securing   (D) security

2. The introduction of the new automated system caused a ------- decrease in errors.

   (A) tragic   (B) frequent   (C) dramatic   (D) powerful

3. Ms. Shin decided to present the results to her boss on ------- own as she felt responsible.

   (A) her   (B) herself   (C) she   (D) hers

4. Our company ------- anonymous satisfaction surveys, and the results were very interesting.

   (A) installed   (B) completed   (C) improved   (D) practiced

5. The training program needs to be translated ------- multiple languages.

   (A) for   (B) at   (C) on   (D) into

6. To develop this product, we need to collaborate with ------- software designers.

   (A) experienced   (B) hesitated   (C) confirmed   (D) inquired

7. Employees can customize and decorate their desk to suit their -------.

   (A) prefers   (B) preferring   (C) preferential   (D) preferences

8. Green Inc. ------- received the Best Office Environmental Award for their office space designs.

   (A) recently   (B) presently   (C) currently   (D) moderately

Part 6

Text Completion

Select the best answer to complete the text. Then choose the letter (A), (B), (C), or (D).

Questions 9-12 refer to the following e-mail.

From: ayakatanaka@whichwaytravel.com

To: staff@whichwaytravel.com

Date: Wednesday, July 11

Subject: Company BBQ

Hello everyone,

This is just another reminder about the company BBQ this month. There is still plenty of time, but please use the link here soon to let us know if you are attending or not. As of now, half of ------ have yet to respond.
9.

It promises to be a good time as always. This year there will be great food and drinks, with games and prizes for workers and their families, and an awards ceremony. Please see the ------ map for location details.
10.

------ you have any questions or concerns about the event, feel free to contact
11.
me.

------.
12.

Ayaka Tanaka

9. (A) helpers   (B) citizens   (C) employees   (D) registrants

10. (A) attach   (B) attached   (C) attaching   (D) attachment

11. (A) While   (B) If   (C) However   (D) And

12. (A) Looking forward to seeing you all there.
    (B) Please tell me more information about the BBQ.
    (C) This event is restricted to certain individuals.
    (D) I'm sorry about the short notice.

Reading Comprehension

Select the best answer for each question and mark the letter (A), (B), (C), or (D).

Questions 13-14 refer to the following advertisement.

Office Planet is collaborating with the world's leading thinkers and designers to apply a greater understanding of people's work habits to create work environments that harness our natural motivations and compel us to produce our best work.

To accommodate the many needs of people doing different work, we propose a shift from standardized workstations and generic meeting rooms to a diverse landscape of purposeful settings. We give individuals something that cannot be had anywhere else: a spiritual connection to work and colleagues; a platform for increased productivity and effectiveness; a more naturally human experience of interaction and creation.

Office Planet Contact us Tel: 808.323.1220 E-mail: contact@office-planet.com

13. What kind of service does Office Planet provide?

(A) Office space consulting

(B) Furniture rentals

(C) Networking services

(D) Meeting spaces

14. According to this advertisement, what can their service provide?

(A) Improved physical health

(B) Better workplace connections

(C) More career prospects

(D) An increase in salary

Questions 15-17 refer to the following memo.

TO: All Employees
FROM: Margaret Wang, HR Director
RE: Attention everyone (especially coffee lovers)

As you know, coffee has been free for all employees ever since we established our company three years ago. Regrettably, there have been several problems associated with this system: arguments over coffee strength; people not cleaning up; people not making a new pot when they finish off the previous pot. There have also been rumors that some people are taking coffee home for personal use.

Consequently, we have no choice but to implement the following new rules:

1. Coffee is no longer free. Every cup of coffee is now 25 cents to be deposited in the black can next to the coffee makers. We suggest you get a supply of quarters for your convenience. This will pay for buying coffee. If the revenue received exceeds the necessary amount, we will have "Free Coffee Fridays" until the surplus is exhausted.

2. Nothing is more frustrating than going for a "cup of joe" only to find the pot empty. Please take the time to make a fresh pot if you finish the previous pot off, especially in the morning when demand is high.

15. How much was a cup of coffee in the past?

(A) It was 25 cents.

(B) It was complimentary.

(C) It was 50 cents.

(D) It depended.

16. What will the company do if there is a surplus of coffee money?

(A) Lower the price

(B) Serve tea

(C) Have free coffee days

(D) Stop serving coffee

17. Which is NOT a problem with the coffee?

(A) Some employees may be stealing it.

(B) It tastes too strong or too weak.

(C) People aren't making new pots.

(D) Employees complain it smells bad.

Recreation

Part 5

Incomplete Sentences

Select the best answer to complete the sentence. Then choose the letter (A), (B), (C), or (D).

1. The committee says athletes should continue preparing for -------.

   (A) competitor   (B) compete   (C) competition   (D) competitive

2. Young composers are urged to submit their newly created -------.

   (A) assignments   (B) licenses   (C) permits   (D) works

3. I ------- with the beautiful scenery on that mountain.

   (A) to impress   (B) impressed   (C) was impressing   (D) was impressed

4. The book event is to take ------- on Saturday morning in the new store.

   (A) over   (B) place   (C) off   (D) advantage

5. Whatever your experience level, our ------- range of fitness classes can help you reach your goal.

   (A) wide   (B) much   (C) rich   (D) long

6. She is wondering ------- she should watch a comedy movie or a horror.

   (A) whether   (B) even   (C) either   (D) both

7. You can join an Adelaide Zoo walk tour every half hour ------- 9 A.M. and 3 P.M.

   (A) at   (B) with   (C) both   (D) between

8. Free brochures with ------- comments from readers will be available at bookstores.

   (A) participation   (B) recommendation   (C) information   (D) portfolio

Part 6

Text Completion

Select the best answer to complete the text. Then choose the letter (A), (B), (C), or (D).

Questions 9-12 refer to the following web page.

Blue Mountain Campground would like to inform you about campground availability this summer. Due to the record rainfall this spring, safety officials have informed us that areas of our campground might be at ------ for landslides.
9.
------ any potential danger, we will be closing these areas immediately. Blue
10.
Mountain Campground will be hiring its own safety inspectors to provide a more detailed safety check and then we will make a decision about our summer schedule ------. ------.
11. **12.**

---

9. (A) danger   (B) chance   (C) accident   (D) risk

10. (A) Avoid   (B) Avoiding   (C) Avoided   (D) To avoid

11. (A) in conclusion   (B) thereafter   (C) lastly   (D) already

12. (A) In the meantime, check the weather report.
    (B) Check this website in the future for further details.
    (C) Cancellation requests will not be accepted.
    (D) Rain or shine, our campground is the best.

Reading Comprehension

Select the best answer for each question and mark the letter (A), (B), (C), or (D).

Questions 13-14 refer to the following notice.

Thank you for your interest in joining the Oakville Tennis Club. Our rates and time schedules are as follows:

• •

Business Hours
Weekdays: 10 a.m. – 10 p.m.
Saturdays: 10 a.m. – 6 p.m.
Sundays and National Holidays: 11 a.m. – 6 p.m.

• •

RATES
Day Pass (Adult $20, Student $10, Child $10, free for children under 6)
Monthly Pass Adult $200, Student $100, Child $100
Tennis Court Rental $10/hr.
Tennis Racket Rental $5

13. How much is a day pass on Tuesday for one adult and two children under 6?

    (A) $20

    (B) $30

    (C) $40

    (D) $50

14. How much would a day pass for four students who use the court for two hours on Saturday?

    (A) $50

    (B) $60

    (C) $70

    (D) $80

Questions 15-17 refer to the following instructions.

Welcome to Erina's Online Piano Course. These lessons are self-paced, hands-on, and very affordable. A live video link allows Erina to give you real time advice and encouragement. Choose any time for your lesson without leaving your own home.

Here's what you will need: an electronic keyboard or piano, access to a computer with a camera and microphone, and the desire to enjoy playing the piano.

If you have any questions during your lessons, click the help button to stop the lesson, and either tell Erina your concern or type her a message. Simple!

15. When are students expected to have lessons?

(A) Every day

(B) Every weekend

(C) Anytime they want to learn

(D) Whenever the instructor is available

16. How can someone ask the teacher a question?

(A) Raise their hand

(B) Call her on the phone

(C) Send her a message

(D) Wave a flag

17. What is NOT required to have lessons?

(A) An electronic keyboard

(B) A computer with some equipment

(C) Some experience to play the piano

(D) The motivation for playing the instrument

Scene 10

Restaurants

Incomplete Sentences

Select the best answer to complete the sentence. Then choose the letter (A), (B), (C), or (D).

1. The new restaurant has a large menu with all-you-can-eat-and-drink -------.
   (A) options   (B) fares   (C) fees   (D) picks

2. Innovative chefs are using ------- produce to create international cuisine.
   (A) locally   (B) local   (C) localized   (D) localize

3. There's a ------- beverage with all lunch menu items.
   (A) supply   (B) contemporary   (C) service   (D) complimentary

4. When I dine alone, I tend ------- to sit at the bar or kitchen counter.
   (A) choose   (B) to choose   (C) has chosen   (D) having been chosen

5. Onuma is a restaurant popular for its ------- products made using fresh milk.
   (A) financial   (B) pure   (C) dairy   (D) industrial

6. That place is known for its ------- Indian cuisine.
   (A) authenticate   (B) authenticity   (C) authentic   (D) authentically

7. That restaurant takes pride in offering only natural products ------- the region.
   (A) upon   (B) from   (C) toward   (D) between

8. The Restaurant Awards ------- added an Asian category since that style became more popular.
   (A) eventually   (B) slightly   (C) considerably   (D) conveniently

Part 6

Text Completion

Select the best answer to complete the text. Then choose the letter (A), (B), (C), or (D).

Questions 9-12 refer to the following letter.

Dear Spaghetti House management,

I am writing this letter to express my sincerest thanks to the Spaghetti House staff working last Thursday, the 17th. They helped make my mother's 70th birthday dinner an ------- event.
9.

We had a reservation for 6 o'clock and soon as we stepped into the restaurant, everyone somehow knew who we were and were wishing my mother a happy birthday. Our server, Greg, was one of the best waitstaff we have ever had. He went out of his way to make sure everything ------- smoothly, from the surprise
10.
cake, to the birthday song and dance by the entire staff. Greg even gave my mother a small wrapped gift as we were leaving. -------, the food was excellent,
11.
as usual.

-------.
12.

Sincerely,

Margaret Chun

---

9. (A) eager   (B) unforgettable   (C) indecisive   (D) unexpected

10. (A) goes   (B) gone   (C) is going   (D) went

11. (A) However   (B) For example   (C) Of course   (D) Therefore

12. (A) Please visit us again for your next birthday.
    (B) In the future, I will be taking my business elsewhere.
    (C) Thank you for a night my mother won't soon forget.
    (D) I hope this birthday dinner will be a success.

Reading Comprehension

Select the best answer for each question and mark the letter (A), (B), (C), or (D).

Questions 13-14 refer to the following receipt.

Wolf Burn's Steakhouse

Date: June 19   Time: 11:31AM
Table: 25   Guest: 2

Dining
1. Cranberry	600
1. Daiquiri	1000
1. WOLF SALAD	1800
1. STEAK FOR TWO	15000
1. MASHED POTATOES	1200
2. Cappuccino @600	1200
1. APPLE STRUDEL	1200

CASH	30000
Subtotal	22000
10% Charge	2200
TAX	1936
Payment	26136
Change Due	3864

* *

Thank you for joining us today.

13. What is NOT shown in this receipt?

(A) Service charge

(B) Tax

(C) Total payment

(D) Tip

14. How many people are probably in this party?

(A) One

(B) Two

(C) Three

(D) Four

Questions 15-16 refer to the following recipe.

Sara's Taco Salad is the perfect treat for Mexican food lovers. It's not too spicy and people on a diet will like it because it's low in fat and high in protein. It is neither expensive nor troublesome to make and can serve 4-6 people. Ideal for parties or as an appetizer.

Ingredients:
1 head of chopped iceberg lettuce
2 large diced tomatoes
1 bunch of chopped green onions
1 can of Maria's Hot Chili Beans
16 oz. of shredded cheddar cheese
1 bag of Sara's Tortilla Chips
1 jar of Harriman's Cream Garlic Salad Dressing

Layer lettuce, green onions and tomatoes in a large bowl. Drain beans in a strainer but do not rinse. Layer the beans on top of the tomatoes. Layer the cheese on top of the beans. Crush Sara's Chips and layer them on top of the cheese. Mix well with dressing, chill in the fridge, then serve. Enjoy!

15. **What is NOT needed to make this taco salad?**
   (A) A bowl
   (B) A knife
   (C) A shredder
   (D) An oven

16. **What should be done before serving?**
   (A) Heat chips in a microwave
   (B) Cool dish in a refrigerator
   (C) Rinse beans thoroughly
   (D) Melt the cheese

Scene 11

Cooking

Part 5

Incomplete Sentences

Select the best answer to complete the sentence. Then choose the letter (A), (B), (C), or (D).

1. Most of the people are interested in buying ------- produced vegetables.
   (A) sustainable   (B) sustain   (C) sustainably   (D) sustainer

2. Asparagus is at its peak from February ------- June.
   (A) on   (B) by   (C) through   (D) at

3. Today's special is chicken that ------- with shrimp.
   (A) were broiled   (C) had broiled
   (B) were being broiled   (D) has been broiled

4. Each recipe is cheaper than fast food, and ------- healthier.
   (A) any   (B) few   (C) much   (D) many

5. The best part of this recipe is how ------- it is to make at home.
   (A) tasty   (B) easy   (C) hungry   (D) local

6. The restaurant critic described the food at Cindy's Cafe as ------- and very authentic.
   (A) affordable   (B) liable   (C) feasible   (D) stable

7. Please help ------- to milk or sugar on the counter over there.
   (A) yourself   (B) you   (C) myself   (D) me

8. Cooking at a higher temperature is the key to making this pizza -------.
   (A) visible   (B) large   (C) perfect   (D) tight

Text Completion

Select the best answer to complete the text. Then choose the letter (A), (B), (C), or (D).

Questions 9-12 refer to the following web page.

Sheridan Cooking College offers a blend of theoretical and practical education, ------- students gain the skills and knowledge to achieve a successful career in
9.

today's food industry. Our ------- learning environments and experiential training
10.

locations are best-in-class. We also offer extensive internship and recruitment

opportunities and a Dean's recognition program to help our students grow their

skills in real world settings. ------- in the heart of downtown Toronto, you are at
11.

the center of the restaurant and food industry in Canada. -------.
12.

---

9. (A) as   (B) to   (C) so   (D) or

10. (A) critical   (B) culinary   (C) cozy   (D) contented

11. (A) Locate   (B) Located   (C) Locating   (D) Is located

12. (A) To find a school near you, please see the information below.
    (B) Call us today to discuss our payment plan options.
    (C) Click here to see more about the restaurants and bars in the area.
    (D) Learn more about our programs by signing up for our newsletter.

Reading Comprehension

Select the best answer for each question and mark the letter (A), (B), (C), or (D).

Questions 13-17 refer to the following article and recipe.

The origins of French toast are not entirely clear, but long before it was called "French toast," similar recipes were being used all around the world. One of the earliest versions of French toast has been traced back to the Roman Empire. The name "French toast" was first used in 17th century England. The recipe — and name — were brought to America by early settlers.

In France, the dish is called "pain perdu," meaning "lost bread." Why lost bread? Originally, people made French toast from stale bread in order to make use of bread that would otherwise have been thrown away.

To make French toast, you first dip slices of bread in a mixture of beaten eggs, milk, cinnamon, and vanilla. Then you fry the egg-coated bread in a pan until browned.

In the United States, restaurants usually serve French toast with butter, maple syrup, or powdered sugar, but the possibilities are endless. French toast can now be seen topped with just about anything Americans can imagine.

It was commonly eaten like pancakes as a breakfast dish but can now be seen eaten at all times of the day in fancy cafes or working-class diners, from the East Coast neighborhoods of New York City to the West Coast communities of Los Angeles.

There are many, fancy variations on this basic recipe. This recipe works with many types of bread — white, whole wheat, cinnamon-raisin, Italian or French. Serve hot with butter, maple syrup and powdered sugar.

by Chef George

Ingredients

Original recipe yields 3 servings

- 6 thick slices of bread
- 2 large eggs
- 2/3 cup milk
- 1/4 teaspoon ground cinnamon
- 1/4 teaspoon ground nutmeg
- 1 teaspoon vanilla extract
- Salt to taste

Direction

1. Beat together egg, milk, salt, desired spices and vanilla.
2. Heat a lightly oiled pan over medium-high heat.
3. Coat each slice of bread in egg mixture, soaking both sides. Place in pan, and cook on both sides until golden. Serve hot.

13. According to the article, what is the origin of French toast?

(A) France   (C) America

(B) England   (D) Unknown

14. Why is French toast called, "lost bread" in France?

(A) People made it from old bread.

(B) People had no idea how to make it at first.

(C) People had difficulty finding the right bread to use.

(D) People used bread that was found on the street.

15. What is inferred about French toast in America?

(A) It is mostly eaten in fast food restaurants.

(B) It is eaten in many different ways.

(C) It is mainly eaten as a breakfast dish.

(D) It is mostly found in the Southern US.

16. In the recipe, the word "beat" in Direction 1, is closest in meaning to

(A) bake   (C) mix

(B) make   (D) toast

17. How many servings is this recipe for?

(A) 2   (C) 4

(B) 3   (D) 6

Travel & Hotels 1

Part 5

Incomplete Sentences

Select the best answer to complete the sentence. Then choose the letter (A), (B), (C), or (D).

1. Whether your flights are booked or you're just planning, here is some ------- advice.

   (A) helpful   (B) help   (C) helping   (D) helped

2. An Asamoah Travel agent will help ------- your trip to your needs and interests.

   (A) tailors   (B) tailoring   (C) tailored   (D) tailor

3. The trains didn't move ------- a snowstorm, so we decided to change our travel plans.

   (A) because   (B) rather   (C) due to   (D) then

4. The airport shuttle bus is always -------, so wait in the lobby a few minutes prior.

   (A) overdue   (B) punctual   (C) affordable   (D) slow

5. Our business is to ------- support and welcome people from all over the world.

   (A) fully   (B) possibly   (C) significantly   (D) uselessly

6. Demand for plane tickets during peak season was in ------- of availability.

   (A) charge   (B) amount   (C) time   (D) excess

7. According to the report, the Star Hotel chain has begun to expand ------- Asia.

   (A) on   (B) at   (C) into   (D) over

8. Our ------- professionals are honored to provide high-quality hospitality.

   (A) experiences   (B) experienced   (C) experience   (D) experiencing

Text Completion

Select the best answer to complete the text. Then choose the letter (A), (B), (C), or (D).

Questions 9-12 refer to the following article.

Room occupancy rates are lower than ------ hotel managers in Orlando had
           9.

expected for this year's American Society of Executive Training (ASET) week.

There are several factors behind the low occupancy, ------ the recent economic
             10.

slowdown.

Hotels depend on corporations sending their HR executives to ASET, but this

year only two thirds of corporate executives attended compared to last year.

------ the economy slowing down, fewer companies are shelling out money to
11.

send their representatives to the big annual event, which can cost more than

8,000 dollars, with some hotels charging 500 dollars a night. ------.
                                                     12.

---

9.   (A) where   (B) which   (C) what   (D) when

10. (A) includes   (B) included   (C) include   (D) including

11. (A) With   (B) For   (C) In   (D) To

12. (A) The unexpected success of this year's event surprised many industry people.
     (B) Recently, training for hotel managers is less of a priority for hotel owners.
     (C) Hotels have been unable to hire staff to meet this year's sudden demand.
     (D) Companies are now looking at cheaper online options for training needs.

Select the best answer for each question and mark the letter (A), (B), (C), or (D).

Questions 13-17 refer to the following website notice and e-mail.

https://www.craneair.com

Crane Airlines Refund policies
We're now offering more options!

If your travel plans have been impacted by the current health crisis and you were scheduled to travel before May 31, you are eligible for a travel coupon that allows you to apply the full value of your ticket to any new flight booked within 24 months.

Depending on the severity of the schedule disruption, you may also be eligible for a refund. Fill out the refund form and we'll contact you shortly to let you know whether your ticket qualifies for a refund. We're experiencing high request volumes due to travel disruptions. Please allow up to 21 business days for your refund request to be processed. If you'd prefer an immediate travel coupon instead, you can claim it **here**.

Check out our refund policies below or go to the Refund FAQ page to learn more about refund eligibility, travel coupon, and cancellation options.

From: michaelmyers@geemail.com
To: representative@craneairlines.com
Date: April 30
Subject: Refund Inquiry

To whom it may concern,

I know you must be very busy at this time. I will get straight to the point. I will not be traveling overseas next month. Actually, due to the recent economic uncertainty, my company is downsizing and, unfortunately, I have been affected by this decision. My company had to let me go, which is fine, as it allows me to pursue other areas of interest.

I see that you have some information about ticket refunds, etc., on your website, but I am confused about one point. I was scheduled to travel on June 1, so will I be eligible for a travel coupon? I would appreciate some information about this, if possible. Also, I assume that the travel coupon is for the final amount paid, including all airport taxes and fees. If this is not the case, please let me know.

As I urgently need to know the answers to these questions, I will continue to call your help number listed on your website.

Thank you for your understanding.

Sincerely,

Michael Myers

13. **What does the notice say about travel coupons?**

    (A) They are issued immediately.

    (B) They can give someone a free flight at any price.

    (C) They can be used for one flight over three years.

    (D) They are valid until May 31.

14. **What does the notice infer about refunds?**

    (A) Full refunds are given to all applicants.

    (B) Refunds are given within one week.

    (C) Some people may be ineligible for a refund.

    (D) Refunds will only be given over the next three weeks.

15. **What is true about Mr. Myers?**

    (A) He works for a travel company.

    (B) He has lost his job.

    (C) He will travel in May.

    (D) He would like to visit a warm climate.

16. **What would Mr. Myers like to know?**

    (A) If his flight is canceled or not

    (B) Where to read about refund policies

    (C) If he will be eligible for a travel coupon

    (D) Who he should contact about changing his flight

17. **What will Mr. Myers most likely do next?**

    (A) Wait for a response to his e-mail

    (B) Call a telephone number

    (C) Read the FAQ webpage

    (D) Fill out the refund form

Office

Part 5

Incomplete Sentences

Select the best answer to complete the sentence. Then choose the letter (A), (B), (C), or (D).

1. Our new copier design has a ------- shape that fits naturally in your office environment.

   (A) simplicity   (B) simply   (C) simplify   (D) simple

2. I'll ask the people who reserved the room ------- they can switch to a room without a projector.

   (A) until   (B) then   (C) however   (D) if

3. Mark managed to set ------- an appointment for us with the well-known architect.

   (A) up   (B) for   (C) about   (D) with

4. We are requested to fill in this form and submit it to ------- supervisor by April 8.

   (A) we   (B) our   (C) us   (D) ourselves

5. If we ------- a document in a shared folder, everyone instantly gets the latest version.

   (A) explore   (B) edit   (C) combine   (D) summarize

6. Any mail sent to our old address will automatically ------- to our new address.

   (A) be forwarded   (B) forwarded   (C) be forwarding   (D) forward

7. Now that we've understood the ------- of the project, let's discuss the details.

   (A) overlook   (B) overview   (C) overtime   (D) overwork

8. Please inform me in advance with ------- what time you'll be arriving.

   (A) thoroughly   (B) approximately   (C) early   (D) minimally

Part 6

Text Completion

Select the best answer to complete the text. Then choose the letter (A), (B), (C), or (D).

Questions 9-12 refer to the following e-mail.

From: mikisato@safewayinsurance.com

To: staff@safewayinsurance.com

Date: Wednesday, October 13

Subject: Halloween Party Info

Hello again,

Sorry for all the e-mails about the Halloween party today. I realized I made a mistake in my previous e-mail. Things will kick off around 6 o'clock in the evening, and NOT 5 o'clock like I ------. Thank you to those who pointed out this error.
  9.

Also, I have received some questions about costumes. It is not ------ to wear a
  10.
costume, ------ we encourage people to try and have some fun. There will be
  11.
some costumes available for those of us with no time to prepare anything.

------. Please let me know by e-mail as soon as possible. Much appreciated.
  12.

Thank you,

Miki Sato

---

9. (A) write (B) written (C) had written (D) am writing

10. (A) customary (B) compulsory (C) careless (D) celebrating

11. (A) however (B) so (C) therefore (D) then

12. (A) I need to know about any mistakes I make.
(B) Please remind me if I forget that you're coming.
(C) The party will take place at some time in the future.
(D) A reminder that I need to know if you can attend or not.

Reading Comprehension

Select the best answer for each question and mark the letter (A), (B), (C), or (D).

Questions 13-17 refer to the following article, e-mail and web page.

Is Video Conferencing Communication Too Much?

10 December — Video conferencing software is now a huge success, with #1 download rankings, status as the main tool for business communication, and being called the technology of the future. So why are some people in business and education finding video conferencing so tiring?

Psychologist Dr. Auston Matthews from Sudbury Hill University says it's because we see ourselves on screen, and want to present a good image to friends and colleagues. "It's likely that this is bringing our self-awareness to a higher level than usual, and therefore we make additional efforts with our appearance," he explains.

Terry Crews, a socio-economist at Walker University says, "It could also be a time issue. We may be scheduling more time using these meetings because we have more time available by staying at home. In order to create a healthier lifestyle, this needs to be reexamined."

Another factor mentioned by many researchers is the extra effort needed to process non-verbal cues such as body language. It's difficult to relax into the conversation naturally when using this type of technology.

From: tonyhawker@geemail.com
To: jennyhawker@geemail.com
Date: January 17
Subject: Job Offer!!!

Hey Jenny,

Congratulations! I heard from your mother about the job offer you received. I think this would be a really good opportunity for you. A promotion to Assistant Professor, even at a small university like Sudbury Hill, is better than continuing to work as a lecturer at Kingston U., unless they offer you a promotion, too. However, if you took the Sudbury Hill job, you'd also be closer to us and could even live here until you found your own apartment. Most importantly, you'd be working in the same department as Dr. Matthews, whom I know you admire and respect.

Anyway, good luck with your decision about your future.

Love,

Dad

---

https://www.westernontariouniversity.com/events

Western Ontario University
Technology Today
One-Day Symposium

Main Hall A, Saturday, October 15, 10:30 A.M. - 4 P.M.

Dr. Nancy Drew (Associate Professor, University of Ancaster)
Virtual Reality vs. Real Reality

Dr. Auston Matthews (Professor, Sudbury Hill University)
Effects of Video Conferencing on the Self

Dr. Kelly Largo (Assistant Professor, University of Grimsby)
The Ego in the Age of Social Media

Dr. Jenny Hawker (Assistant Professor, Kingston University)
The Old Man and the Cell: The Elderly and Social Media

For more information and to register, go to www.americanpsychologytoday.com/conference

13. **What does the article imply about video conferencing technology?**

   (A) It is the future of communication.

   (B) Relying on it a lot can be tiring for people.

   (C) The membership plans can be expensive.

   (D) There are too many problems with security.

14. **What does Mr. Crews say needs to be reexamined?**

   (A) The way companies choose technology

   (B) How people appear on video

   (C) The way people speak on camera

   (D) The length of time spent in video conferencing

15. **What most likely is Ms. Hawker's research area?**

   (A) Business

   (B) Education

   (C) Psychology

   (D) Socio-economics

16. **What is the purpose of this web page?**

   (A) To promote a special event

   (B) To announce new faculty

   (C) To provide information about a school

   (D) To show recent social trends

17. **What is most likely true about Ms. Hawker?**

   (A) She recently changed her schools.

   (B) She received a promotion at her workplace.

   (C) She works with Dr. Matthews.

   (D) She lives with her parents.

Travel & Hotels 2

Part 5

Incomplete Sentences

Select the best answer to complete the sentence. Then choose the letter (A), (B), (C), or (D).

1. Melia Hotel is ------- located for both business and leisure guests in Ibiza.

   (A) perfectly   (B) elegantly   (C) only   (D) quietly

2. The SHO Hotel is the best ------- point from which to explore London.

   (A) start   (B) to start   (C) started   (D) starting

3. Whether you are traveling on business or on holiday, our rooms are designed to ------- your needs.

   (A) get   (B) meet   (C) catch   (D) have

4. All guests enjoy ------- wireless Internet access.

   (A) limited   (B) unlimited   (C) limiting   (D) limit

5. It is recommended that you visit the islands ------- by the beautiful sea.

   (A) visited   (B) located   (C) placed   (D) surrounded

6. ------- significant damage from the earthquake, the city is functioning well again.

   (A) Throughout   (B) Besides   (C) Despite   (D) Due to

7. Each guestroom ------- with handy amenities.

   (A) equipped   (B) is equipped   (C) equips   (D) is equipping

8. This safari tour provides a private vehicle and a driver ------- camping equipment.

   (A) next to   (B) out of   (C) along with   (D) about to

Text Completion

Select the best answer to complete the text. Then choose the letter (A), (B), (C), or (D).

Questions 9-12 refer to the following website.

With credit card travel points, you should always try to maximize for value. That means making sure you get ------ out of your hard-earned points. Whether **9.** you use your rewards to book your travel directly, exchange them for cash back, or transfer them over to a ------ airline or hotel program, you should **10.** generally try and get at least $0.01 per point. ------, other factors may impact **11.** this number. ------. This guide will walk you through everything you need to **12.** know about using your credit card points.

9. (A) best　　　(B) enough　　(C) sufficient　　(D) higher

10. (A) participate　　(B) participated　　(C) participation　　(D) participating

11. (A) Still　　　(B) Anyway　　(C) However　　(D) Otherwise

12. (A) Become familiar with these influences and adjust your expectations accordingly.
    (B) Try and spend as much money as possible to get lots of points and rewards.
    (C) These factors are difficult to know, so ignore them, and enjoy your shopping experience.
    (D) Apply for your USA Express credit card and receive bonus points today!

Reading Comprehension

Select the best answer for each question and mark the letter (A), (B), (C), or (D).

Questions 13-17 refer to the following article, notice and e-mail.

What's Old is New Again

3 November — Most of us know The Old Hampton Inn; the popular tourist attraction in downtown Stoney Creek. Established in 1843, it has seen its share of owners over the years. A group of investors looking to capitalize on the hotel's fame purchased the hotel last year. After undergoing a multi-million-dollar renovation, the new Old Hampton Inn will finally have a grand reopening ceremony this Friday. Those people rumored to be at the event are the mayor and local celebrities and athletes. Previous owner Agatha Black stated, "It's good to see the old hotel looking beautiful again." But went on to say that the new owners should not try to raise prices as a way to make some quick money. "The hotel is a piece of history and should be experienced by everyone. Not just those with lots of money. I would hate to see that change."

Attention Freddy's Diner Staff

The annual drink-sales promotion is upon us again. Sell the most drinks this week and win prizes. Get all the details from either the day manager, Mark, or the night manager, Greg.

The promotion will begin with this Monday's lunch service and finish with Sunday's evening service.

1st Prize: One night at the newly renovated The Old Hampton Inn
(valued at over $600!!!)
2nd Prize: Two tickets to a Blue Socks baseball game ($90 value)
3rd Prize: A 1.5 liter bottle of St. Verger Champagne ($70 value)
4th Prize: A coupon for a massage at Tender Touch ($50 value)

I don't know about you, but this year's 1st prize is extremely attractive since The Old Hampton Inn is not as affordable as it once was. A big thank you to our neighbor's The Old Hampton Inn and its mysterious new owners for being so generous.

Good luck everyone!

From: sachichiba@geemail.com
To: gregwallace@freddysdiner.com
Date: January 5
Subject: The Prize

Hey Greg,

Thanks for letting me know the result of the contest. To be honest, I don't think I should get the prize. The reason I sold so many drinks was because I served those two big parties early in the week. Hannah got the 4th prize but worked so much harder than me, so if you don't mind, could we trade prizes? I'm not much of a drinker anyway. I know we could just trade the prizes, but it'd be better if it was done officially by you, or Mark. Anyway, I'm sure we'd all like to trade prizes with Amanda. This is the only way any of us would be able to stay there, as it's so expensive now. Lucky girl!

Sachi

13. **What is the main purpose of the article?**

(A) To advertise a hotel tour package

(B) To promote a new business plan

(C) To offer a discount on hotel stays

(D) To announce an event at a local business

14. **What does Ms. Black say the owners should be careful about?**

(A) Inviting so many people to the opening

(B) Spending too much money on repairs

(C) Charging guests a lot of money

(D) Letting too many people inside the building

15. **Where would this notice most likely be seen?**

(A) In the lobby of a hotel

(B) Inside restaurant menus

(C) In the local newspaper

(D) On a restaurant staffroom wall

16. **What is most likely true about the owners of The Old Hampton Inn?**

(A) They visit local restaurants regularly.

(B) They have increased the hotel prices.

(C) They know their neighbors personally.

(D) They will compete in the sales promotion.

17. **What prize did Sachi win?**

(A) A night at The Old Hampton Inn

(B) Baseball tickets

(C) A bottle of champagne

(D) A massage coupon

General

Part 5

Incomplete Sentences

Select the best answer to complete the sentence. Then choose the letter (A), (B), (C), or (D).

1. All opposition to this new plan -------.

   (A) collapse   (B) collapsed   (C) was collapsed   (D) was collapsing

2. The summary court is located on Benton Street, directly ------- from Glenview Station.

   (A) across   (B) among   (C) apart   (D) nearby

3. Our company has a special ------- to pay for employee medical emergencies.

   (A) domain   (B) bank   (C) custom   (D) fund

4. The Philippines economic growth rate has been ------- increasing in recent years.

   (A) steadiness   (B) steadying   (C) steadily   (D) steadied

5. ------- accordance with the law, smoking will be prohibited in all our facilities.

   (A) In   (B) Once   (C) Soon   (D) By

6. We handle a wide range of legal -------, including local and international matters.

   (A) disputes   (B) disputed   (C) dispute   (D) disputing

7. The ------- age for national elections was lowered to 18 from 20 years old.

   (A) agreeing   (B) voting   (C) playing   (D) selecting

8. The government will impose ------- controls on foreign goods.

   (A) strictest   (B) strictness   (C) strictly   (D) strict

Part 6

Text Completion

Select the best answer to complete the text. Then choose the letter (A), (B), (C), or (D).

Questions 9-12 refer to the following web page.

The Sakura Hotel in NYC offers tradition and luxury with professional staff. It is our attention to detail that sets The Sakura ------ from other hotels, giving you
9.
a perfect New York City experience. As a guest of The Sakura, you have the opportunity to experience what one of the highest-rated hotels in New York City has ------. ------, we put you in the ideal location for exploring New York City's
10. **11.**
most famous areas. ------. World-famous museums, shops, and restaurants are
12.
also within walking distance of the hotel.

9. (A) away   (B) along   (C) around   (D) apart

10. (A) to include   (B) to offer   (C) to realize   (D) to find

11. (A) Nonetheless   (B) Yet   (C) Conversely   (D) Additionally

12. (A) You're just steps away from places like Central Park and Times Square.
   (B) Our staff will direct you to the nearest train station to get to the city.
   (C) To find a location near you, please click the link below.
   (D) Please complete the feedback form about your recent stay with us.

Reading Comprehension

Select the best answer for each question and mark the letter (A), (B), (C), or (D).

Questions 13-17 refer to the following schedule and e-mails.

Rebirth Sports Club: Basic Yoga Schedule May						
Sunday	Monday	Tuesday	Wednesday	Thursday	Friday	Saturday
			closed 1	closed 2	3	16:00 Miku 4
closed 5	6	10:00 Miku 7	8	9	15:00 Atsuko 10	11
closed 12	13	10:00 Miku 14	15	16	17	13:00 Miku 18
closed 19	20	10:00 Miku 21	22	23	TBD 24	TBD 25
closed 26	27	14:00 Atsuko 28	29	30	31	

From: sarahparker@geemail.com

To: frontdesk@rebirthsportsclub.com

Date: April 14

Subject: Yoga Class

Hello,

I have a question regarding the Basic Yoga class offered at your sports club. I pay to take four classes a month, but looking at the May schedule, it looks like I'll just be able to take three classes. I can only take morning classes during the week, as I have to pick up my kids in the afternoons, and then I'm busy on weekends driving them to soccer practice. Will I get reimbursed for the missing class or can I use it in June?

By the way, I feel that there should be more scheduling options for taking classes. It looks like there are less and less classes available each month, which is unfair for people like me with limited free time.

Thank you,

Sarah Parker

From: frontdesk@rebirthsportsclub.com

To: sarahparker@geemail.com

Date: April 16

Subject: RE: Yoga Class

Dear Ms. Parker,

Thank you for taking the time to write us. You'll be happy to know that the TBD ("To Be Decided") class will take place at 11:00 and will be conducted by your regular instructor, Miku.

Unfortunately, we don't allow guests to take unused classes in the following month, so if you are unable to attend this newly scheduled class, please let me know, and I'll proceed to refund you the equivalent of one class.

I would also recommend that you fill in a feedback form located at the club reception desk about the scheduling of classes. Upper management get these written forms directly, and they seem to take club members' opinions very seriously.

Feel free to contact me about anything in the future.

Sincerely,

Michelle O'Brian
Front Desk
Rebirth Sports Club

13. Which class is Ms. Parker able to attend?

    (A) May 4

    (B) May 10

    (C) May 21

    (D) May 28

14. What is indicated about Ms. Parker?

    (A) She is a soccer coach.

    (B) She works in the evenings.

    (C) She has a full time job.

    (D) She has children.

15. What does Ms. Parker say about the schedule?

    (A) There are too many classes taught by Miku.

    (B) It should have a greater variety of instructors.

    (C) There are too many "To Be Decided" classes.

    (D) It should have more classes available.

16. What is recommended that Ms. Parker do about her missed class?

    (A) Take the class on May 24

    (B) Take the class in June

    (C) Ask her instructor to change the time

    (D) Ask management for a special class

17. What does Ms. O'Brian suggest Ms. Parker do about her complaint?

    (A) Call the Front Desk

    (B) Submit her opinion in writing

    (C) Talk to somebody in management directly

    (D) Consider canceling her membership

Scene 4

DATE   /   /

1. Ⓐ Ⓑ Ⓒ Ⓓ   9. Ⓐ Ⓑ Ⓒ Ⓓ
2. Ⓐ Ⓑ Ⓒ Ⓓ   10. Ⓐ Ⓑ Ⓒ Ⓓ
3. Ⓐ Ⓑ Ⓒ Ⓓ   11. Ⓐ Ⓑ Ⓒ Ⓓ
4. Ⓐ Ⓑ Ⓒ Ⓓ   12. Ⓐ Ⓑ Ⓒ Ⓓ
5. Ⓐ Ⓑ Ⓒ Ⓓ   13. Ⓐ Ⓑ Ⓒ Ⓓ
6. Ⓐ Ⓑ Ⓒ Ⓓ   14. Ⓐ Ⓑ Ⓒ Ⓓ
7. Ⓐ Ⓑ Ⓒ Ⓓ   15. Ⓐ Ⓑ Ⓒ Ⓓ
8. Ⓐ Ⓑ Ⓒ Ⓓ   16. Ⓐ Ⓑ Ⓒ Ⓓ

STUDENT ID _____

NAME _____

TODAY'S SCORE

Scene 1

DATE   /   /

1. Ⓐ Ⓑ Ⓒ Ⓓ   9. Ⓐ Ⓑ Ⓒ Ⓓ
2. Ⓐ Ⓑ Ⓒ Ⓓ   10. Ⓐ Ⓑ Ⓒ Ⓓ
3. Ⓐ Ⓑ Ⓒ Ⓓ   11. Ⓐ Ⓑ Ⓒ Ⓓ
4. Ⓐ Ⓑ Ⓒ Ⓓ   12. Ⓐ Ⓑ Ⓒ Ⓓ
5. Ⓐ Ⓑ Ⓒ Ⓓ   13. Ⓐ Ⓑ Ⓒ Ⓓ
6. Ⓐ Ⓑ Ⓒ Ⓓ   14. Ⓐ Ⓑ Ⓒ Ⓓ
7. Ⓐ Ⓑ Ⓒ Ⓓ   15. Ⓐ Ⓑ Ⓒ Ⓓ
8. Ⓐ Ⓑ Ⓒ Ⓓ   16. Ⓐ Ⓑ Ⓒ Ⓓ
                     17. Ⓐ Ⓑ Ⓒ Ⓓ

STUDENT ID _____

NAME _____

TODAY'S SCORE

Scene 5

DATE   /   /

1. Ⓐ Ⓑ Ⓒ Ⓓ   9. Ⓐ Ⓑ Ⓒ Ⓓ
2. Ⓐ Ⓑ Ⓒ Ⓓ   10. Ⓐ Ⓑ Ⓒ Ⓓ
3. Ⓐ Ⓑ Ⓒ Ⓓ   11. Ⓐ Ⓑ Ⓒ Ⓓ
4. Ⓐ Ⓑ Ⓒ Ⓓ   12. Ⓐ Ⓑ Ⓒ Ⓓ
5. Ⓐ Ⓑ Ⓒ Ⓓ   13. Ⓐ Ⓑ Ⓒ Ⓓ
6. Ⓐ Ⓑ Ⓒ Ⓓ   14. Ⓐ Ⓑ Ⓒ Ⓓ
7. Ⓐ Ⓑ Ⓒ Ⓓ   15. Ⓐ Ⓑ Ⓒ Ⓓ
8. Ⓐ Ⓑ Ⓒ Ⓓ   16. Ⓐ Ⓑ Ⓒ Ⓓ

STUDENT ID _____

NAME _____

TODAY'S SCORE

Scene 2

DATE   /   /

1. Ⓐ Ⓑ Ⓒ Ⓓ   9. Ⓐ Ⓑ Ⓒ Ⓓ
2. Ⓐ Ⓑ Ⓒ Ⓓ   10. Ⓐ Ⓑ Ⓒ Ⓓ
3. Ⓐ Ⓑ Ⓒ Ⓓ   11. Ⓐ Ⓑ Ⓒ Ⓓ
4. Ⓐ Ⓑ Ⓒ Ⓓ   12. Ⓐ Ⓑ Ⓒ Ⓓ
5. Ⓐ Ⓑ Ⓒ Ⓓ   13. Ⓐ Ⓑ Ⓒ Ⓓ
6. Ⓐ Ⓑ Ⓒ Ⓓ   14. Ⓐ Ⓑ Ⓒ Ⓓ
7. Ⓐ Ⓑ Ⓒ Ⓓ   15. Ⓐ Ⓑ Ⓒ Ⓓ
8. Ⓐ Ⓑ Ⓒ Ⓓ   16. Ⓐ Ⓑ Ⓒ Ⓓ

STUDENT ID _____

NAME _____

TODAY'S SCORE

Scene 6

DATE   /   /

1. Ⓐ Ⓑ Ⓒ Ⓓ   9. Ⓐ Ⓑ Ⓒ Ⓓ
2. Ⓐ Ⓑ Ⓒ Ⓓ   10. Ⓐ Ⓑ Ⓒ Ⓓ
3. Ⓐ Ⓑ Ⓒ Ⓓ   11. Ⓐ Ⓑ Ⓒ Ⓓ
4. Ⓐ Ⓑ Ⓒ Ⓓ   12. Ⓐ Ⓑ Ⓒ Ⓓ
5. Ⓐ Ⓑ Ⓒ Ⓓ   13. Ⓐ Ⓑ Ⓒ Ⓓ
6. Ⓐ Ⓑ Ⓒ Ⓓ   14. Ⓐ Ⓑ Ⓒ Ⓓ
7. Ⓐ Ⓑ Ⓒ Ⓓ   15. Ⓐ Ⓑ Ⓒ Ⓓ
8. Ⓐ Ⓑ Ⓒ Ⓓ   16. Ⓐ Ⓑ Ⓒ Ⓓ

STUDENT ID _____

NAME _____

TODAY'S SCORE

Scene 3

DATE   /   /

1. Ⓐ Ⓑ Ⓒ Ⓓ   9. Ⓐ Ⓑ Ⓒ Ⓓ
2. Ⓐ Ⓑ Ⓒ Ⓓ   10. Ⓐ Ⓑ Ⓒ Ⓓ
3. Ⓐ Ⓑ Ⓒ Ⓓ   11. Ⓐ Ⓑ Ⓒ Ⓓ
4. Ⓐ Ⓑ Ⓒ Ⓓ   12. Ⓐ Ⓑ Ⓒ Ⓓ
5. Ⓐ Ⓑ Ⓒ Ⓓ   13. Ⓐ Ⓑ Ⓒ Ⓓ
6. Ⓐ Ⓑ Ⓒ Ⓓ   14. Ⓐ Ⓑ Ⓒ Ⓓ
7. Ⓐ Ⓑ Ⓒ Ⓓ   15. Ⓐ Ⓑ Ⓒ Ⓓ
8. Ⓐ Ⓑ Ⓒ Ⓓ   16. Ⓐ Ⓑ Ⓒ Ⓓ

STUDENT ID _____

NAME _____

TODAY'S SCORE

Scene 10

DATE ___ / ___ / ___

1. Ⓐ Ⓑ Ⓒ Ⓓ   9. Ⓐ Ⓑ Ⓒ Ⓓ
2. Ⓐ Ⓑ Ⓒ Ⓓ   10. Ⓐ Ⓑ Ⓒ Ⓓ
3. Ⓐ Ⓑ Ⓒ Ⓓ   11. Ⓐ Ⓑ Ⓒ Ⓓ
4. Ⓐ Ⓑ Ⓒ Ⓓ   12. Ⓐ Ⓑ Ⓒ Ⓓ
5. Ⓐ Ⓑ Ⓒ Ⓓ   13. Ⓐ Ⓑ Ⓒ Ⓓ
6. Ⓐ Ⓑ Ⓒ Ⓓ   14. Ⓐ Ⓑ Ⓒ Ⓓ
7. Ⓐ Ⓑ Ⓒ Ⓓ   15. Ⓐ Ⓑ Ⓒ Ⓓ
8. Ⓐ Ⓑ Ⓒ Ⓓ   16. Ⓐ Ⓑ Ⓒ Ⓓ

STUDENT ID _____

NAME _____

TODAY'S SCORE

Scene 7

DATE ___ / ___ / ___

1. Ⓐ Ⓑ Ⓒ Ⓓ   9. Ⓐ Ⓑ Ⓒ Ⓓ
2. Ⓐ Ⓑ Ⓒ Ⓓ   10. Ⓐ Ⓑ Ⓒ Ⓓ
3. Ⓐ Ⓑ Ⓒ Ⓓ   11. Ⓐ Ⓑ Ⓒ Ⓓ
4. Ⓐ Ⓑ Ⓒ Ⓓ   12. Ⓐ Ⓑ Ⓒ Ⓓ
5. Ⓐ Ⓑ Ⓒ Ⓓ   13. Ⓐ Ⓑ Ⓒ Ⓓ
6. Ⓐ Ⓑ Ⓒ Ⓓ   14. Ⓐ Ⓑ Ⓒ Ⓓ
7. Ⓐ Ⓑ Ⓒ Ⓓ   15. Ⓐ Ⓑ Ⓒ Ⓓ
8. Ⓐ Ⓑ Ⓒ Ⓓ   16. Ⓐ Ⓑ Ⓒ Ⓓ

STUDENT ID _____

NAME _____

TODAY'S SCORE

Scene 11

DATE ___ / ___ / ___

1. Ⓐ Ⓑ Ⓒ Ⓓ   9. Ⓐ Ⓑ Ⓒ Ⓓ
2. Ⓐ Ⓑ Ⓒ Ⓓ   10. Ⓐ Ⓑ Ⓒ Ⓓ
3. Ⓐ Ⓑ Ⓒ Ⓓ   11. Ⓐ Ⓑ Ⓒ Ⓓ
4. Ⓐ Ⓑ Ⓒ Ⓓ   12. Ⓐ Ⓑ Ⓒ Ⓓ
5. Ⓐ Ⓑ Ⓒ Ⓓ   13. Ⓐ Ⓑ Ⓒ Ⓓ
6. Ⓐ Ⓑ Ⓒ Ⓓ   14. Ⓐ Ⓑ Ⓒ Ⓓ
7. Ⓐ Ⓑ Ⓒ Ⓓ   15. Ⓐ Ⓑ Ⓒ Ⓓ
8. Ⓐ Ⓑ Ⓒ Ⓓ   16. Ⓐ Ⓑ Ⓒ Ⓓ
                 17. Ⓐ Ⓑ Ⓒ Ⓓ

STUDENT ID _____

NAME _____

TODAY'S SCORE

Scene 8

DATE ___ / ___ / ___

1. Ⓐ Ⓑ Ⓒ Ⓓ   9. Ⓐ Ⓑ Ⓒ Ⓓ
2. Ⓐ Ⓑ Ⓒ Ⓓ   10. Ⓐ Ⓑ Ⓒ Ⓓ
3. Ⓐ Ⓑ Ⓒ Ⓓ   11. Ⓐ Ⓑ Ⓒ Ⓓ
4. Ⓐ Ⓑ Ⓒ Ⓓ   12. Ⓐ Ⓑ Ⓒ Ⓓ
5. Ⓐ Ⓑ Ⓒ Ⓓ   13. Ⓐ Ⓑ Ⓒ Ⓓ
6. Ⓐ Ⓑ Ⓒ Ⓓ   14. Ⓐ Ⓑ Ⓒ Ⓓ
7. Ⓐ Ⓑ Ⓒ Ⓓ   15. Ⓐ Ⓑ Ⓒ Ⓓ
8. Ⓐ Ⓑ Ⓒ Ⓓ   16. Ⓐ Ⓑ Ⓒ Ⓓ
                 17. Ⓐ Ⓑ Ⓒ Ⓓ

STUDENT ID _____

NAME _____

TODAY'S SCORE

Scene 12

DATE ___ / ___ / ___

1. Ⓐ Ⓑ Ⓒ Ⓓ   9. Ⓐ Ⓑ Ⓒ Ⓓ
2. Ⓐ Ⓑ Ⓒ Ⓓ   10. Ⓐ Ⓑ Ⓒ Ⓓ
3. Ⓐ Ⓑ Ⓒ Ⓓ   11. Ⓐ Ⓑ Ⓒ Ⓓ
4. Ⓐ Ⓑ Ⓒ Ⓓ   12. Ⓐ Ⓑ Ⓒ Ⓓ
5. Ⓐ Ⓑ Ⓒ Ⓓ   13. Ⓐ Ⓑ Ⓒ Ⓓ
6. Ⓐ Ⓑ Ⓒ Ⓓ   14. Ⓐ Ⓑ Ⓒ Ⓓ
7. Ⓐ Ⓑ Ⓒ Ⓓ   15. Ⓐ Ⓑ Ⓒ Ⓓ
8. Ⓐ Ⓑ Ⓒ Ⓓ   16. Ⓐ Ⓑ Ⓒ Ⓓ
                 17. Ⓐ Ⓑ Ⓒ Ⓓ

STUDENT ID _____

NAME _____

TODAY'S SCORE

Scene 9

DATE ___ / ___ / ___

1. Ⓐ Ⓑ Ⓒ Ⓓ   9. Ⓐ Ⓑ Ⓒ Ⓓ
2. Ⓐ Ⓑ Ⓒ Ⓓ   10. Ⓐ Ⓑ Ⓒ Ⓓ
3. Ⓐ Ⓑ Ⓒ Ⓓ   11. Ⓐ Ⓑ Ⓒ Ⓓ
4. Ⓐ Ⓑ Ⓒ Ⓓ   12. Ⓐ Ⓑ Ⓒ Ⓓ
5. Ⓐ Ⓑ Ⓒ Ⓓ   13. Ⓐ Ⓑ Ⓒ Ⓓ
6. Ⓐ Ⓑ Ⓒ Ⓓ   14. Ⓐ Ⓑ Ⓒ Ⓓ
7. Ⓐ Ⓑ Ⓒ Ⓓ   15. Ⓐ Ⓑ Ⓒ Ⓓ
8. Ⓐ Ⓑ Ⓒ Ⓓ   16. Ⓐ Ⓑ Ⓒ Ⓓ
                 17. Ⓐ Ⓑ Ⓒ Ⓓ

STUDENT ID _____

NAME _____

TODAY'S SCORE

Scene 13

DATE ___ / ___ / ___

1. Ⓐ Ⓑ Ⓒ Ⓓ	**9.** Ⓐ Ⓑ Ⓒ Ⓓ
2. Ⓐ Ⓑ Ⓒ Ⓓ	**10.** Ⓐ Ⓑ Ⓒ Ⓓ
3. Ⓐ Ⓑ Ⓒ Ⓓ	**11.** Ⓐ Ⓑ Ⓒ Ⓓ
4. Ⓐ Ⓑ Ⓒ Ⓓ	**12.** Ⓐ Ⓑ Ⓒ Ⓓ
5. Ⓐ Ⓑ Ⓒ Ⓓ	**13.** Ⓐ Ⓑ Ⓒ Ⓓ
6. Ⓐ Ⓑ Ⓒ Ⓓ	**14.** Ⓐ Ⓑ Ⓒ Ⓓ
7. Ⓐ Ⓑ Ⓒ Ⓓ	**15.** Ⓐ Ⓑ Ⓒ Ⓓ
8. Ⓐ Ⓑ Ⓒ Ⓓ	**16.** Ⓐ Ⓑ Ⓒ Ⓓ
	17. Ⓐ Ⓑ Ⓒ Ⓓ

STUDENT ID ___

NAME ___

TODAY'S SCORE

Scene 14

DATE ___ / ___ / ___

1. Ⓐ Ⓑ Ⓒ Ⓓ	**9.** Ⓐ Ⓑ Ⓒ Ⓓ
2. Ⓐ Ⓑ Ⓒ Ⓓ	**10.** Ⓐ Ⓑ Ⓒ Ⓓ
3. Ⓐ Ⓑ Ⓒ Ⓓ	**11.** Ⓐ Ⓑ Ⓒ Ⓓ
4. Ⓐ Ⓑ Ⓒ Ⓓ	**12.** Ⓐ Ⓑ Ⓒ Ⓓ
5. Ⓐ Ⓑ Ⓒ Ⓓ	**13.** Ⓐ Ⓑ Ⓒ Ⓓ
6. Ⓐ Ⓑ Ⓒ Ⓓ	**14.** Ⓐ Ⓑ Ⓒ Ⓓ
7. Ⓐ Ⓑ Ⓒ Ⓓ	**15.** Ⓐ Ⓑ Ⓒ Ⓓ
8. Ⓐ Ⓑ Ⓒ Ⓓ	**16.** Ⓐ Ⓑ Ⓒ Ⓓ
	17. Ⓐ Ⓑ Ⓒ Ⓓ

STUDENT ID ___

NAME ___

TODAY'S SCORE

Scene 15

DATE ___ / ___ / ___

1. Ⓐ Ⓑ Ⓒ Ⓓ	**9.** Ⓐ Ⓑ Ⓒ Ⓓ
2. Ⓐ Ⓑ Ⓒ Ⓓ	**10.** Ⓐ Ⓑ Ⓒ Ⓓ
3. Ⓐ Ⓑ Ⓒ Ⓓ	**11.** Ⓐ Ⓑ Ⓒ Ⓓ
4. Ⓐ Ⓑ Ⓒ Ⓓ	**12.** Ⓐ Ⓑ Ⓒ Ⓓ
5. Ⓐ Ⓑ Ⓒ Ⓓ	**13.** Ⓐ Ⓑ Ⓒ Ⓓ
6. Ⓐ Ⓑ Ⓒ Ⓓ	**14.** Ⓐ Ⓑ Ⓒ Ⓓ
7. Ⓐ Ⓑ Ⓒ Ⓓ	**15.** Ⓐ Ⓑ Ⓒ Ⓓ
8. Ⓐ Ⓑ Ⓒ Ⓓ	**16.** Ⓐ Ⓑ Ⓒ Ⓓ
	17. Ⓐ Ⓑ Ⓒ Ⓓ

STUDENT ID ___

NAME ___

TODAY'S SCORE

PROFILE／著者略歴

Matthew Wilson（マシュー・ウィルソン）

宮城大学基盤教育群教授。
カナダ・トロント出身。カナダ、韓国、日本で長年、英語教育に携わる。仙台市教育委員会教育アドバイザーを経て2009年より宮城大学事業構想学部准教授、2016年より同教授、2017年より現職。研究分野は日本における英語教育と学生の動機づけ。米国のシェナンドア大学大学院卒業。同校より修士号取得 (TESOL)。

鶴岡 公幸（つるおか ともゆき）

神田外語大学外国語学部教授。
神奈川県横浜市出身。キッコーマン (株)、(財) 国際ビジネスコミュニケーション協会、KPMGあずさ監査法人、宮城大学食産業学部を経て、2014年より現職。1998年インディアナ大学経営大学院卒業。同校より経営学修士 (MBA) 取得。専門はマーケティング、ビジネス英語。TOEIC®関連書籍を含め著書、テキスト多数。

佐藤 千春（さとう ちはる）

株式会社and ENGLISH代表取締役。
山形県出身。岩手大学人文社会科学部卒業。山形県公立中学校英語教諭として14年間勤務。社会教育主事補資格取得。退職後、都内TOEIC®専門校講師兼マネージャーとしての勤務を経て、英語スクール『株式会社and ENGLISH』を起業。編集協力としてTOEIC®単語集の出版に携わる。

QUICK EXERCISES FOR THE TOEIC® L&R TEST 500 Reading
切り取り提出式 スコア別 TOEIC® L&R徹底対策ドリル500 リーディング編

2021年4月5日　初版第1刷発行

著　　者　Matthew Wilson／鶴岡公幸／佐藤千春

発行者　森　信久
発行所　**株式会社　松 柏 社**
　　　　〒102-0072　東京都千代田区飯田橋1-6-1
　　　　TEL　03 (3230) 4813（代表）
　　　　FAX　03 (3230) 4857
　　　　http://www.shohakusha.com
　　　　e-mail: info@shohakusha.com

装　　幀　小島トシノブ（NONdesign）
本文レイアウト・組版　赤木健太郎（有限会社ケークルーデザインワークス）
印刷・製本　シナノ書籍印刷株式会社
ISBN978-4-88198-765-0
略号＝765
Copyright © 2021 by Matthew Wilson, Tomoyuki Tsuruoka and Chiharu Sato